Snippets of Nigel Farage

Dave Farnham

Copyright © 2014 Dave Farnham
All rights reserved.

ISBN-13: 13: 978-1497498426
ISBN-10: 1497498422

Other books by Dave Farnham

Snippets of Abraham Lincoln

Snippets of Benjamin Franklin

Snippets of Billy Connolly

Snippets of Boris Johnson

Snippets of Jealousy

Snippets of Jeremy Kyle

Snippets of Joan Rivers

Snippets of Oscar Wilde

Snippets of Marilyn Monroe

Snippets of Paul Gascoigne

Snippets of Richard Attenborough

Snippets of Vladimir Putin

Snippets of Love

Snippets of Success

Gandhi's Teachings for Troubled Times

Disclaimer:

While every effort has been made to ensure the information in this book is correct, human error is always a possibility and therefore the author cannot accept responsibility for any inaccuracies.

A Brief Introduction

Love him or hate him, Nigel Farage is one of those rare breeds of politician you can't help but pay keen attention to, always wondering what will come out of his mouth next. Not one to mince his words, Farage has risen from the political shadows to become a household name.

Wonderful or blunderful? That's for you to decide. Here are some of the best snippets about and by the man himself.

Nigel Farage - Curriculum Vitae

Nationality: British

Born: April 3 1964

Background: Herne in Kent, son of Guy Justus Oscar Farage, a stockbroker.

Educated: Dulwich College, a private school in south London.

Marital status: Married twice with four children. Second wife, Kirsten Mehr, a former bond dealer, is German.

Employment: Earned £200,000 as a commodity broker at 21. Stood six times for election as MP. UKIP leader twice. MEP since 1999.

Health: A smoker. "You are only here once," he says.

Belief: An agnostic: "I think there is something there, but that's as far as it goes."

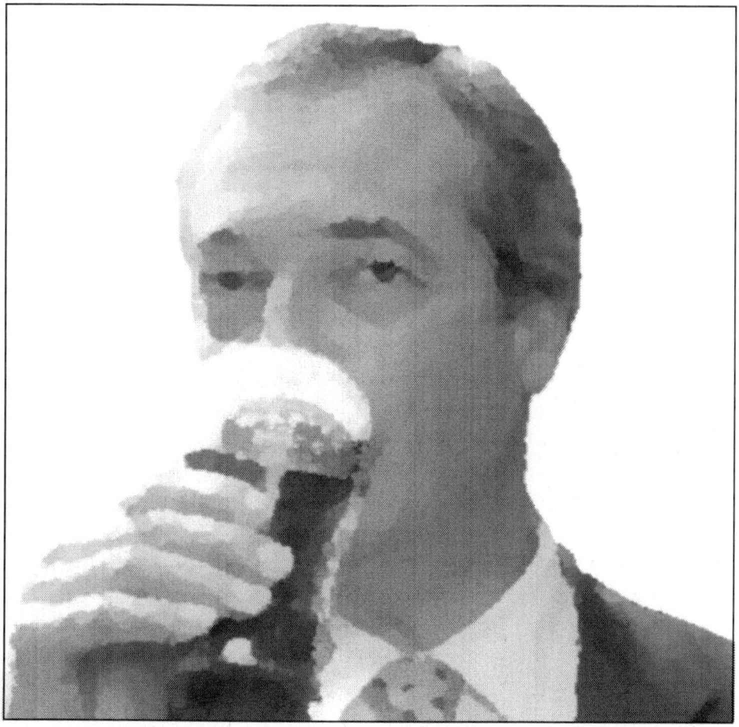

"I approve of Jesus. He seems a decent sort who liked his wine and the company of riff-raff."

Nigel Farage

Speaking to Herman Van Rompuy, President of the EU:

"You have the charisma of a damp rag and the appearance of a low grade bank clerk. And the question that I wanna ask, that we're all gonna ask is: who are you? I'd never heard of you, nobody in Europe'd ever heard of you. I would like to ask you, President, who voted for you?"

Nigel Farage

Mr Farage said new policies would be "similar in flavour" to his past manifesto pledges which included bringing in a dress code for taxi drivers, repainting trains traditional colours and introducing a dress code for taxi drivers.

Georgia Graham, The Telegraph

While on BBC Radio 4's Today programme, Mr Farage was questioned about why he had told the President of the European Council, Herman Van Rompuy, that he had the "charisma of a damp rag."

"What does being so rude achieve?" Mr Farage was asked.

"Well, it has got me on this programme, hasn't it?"

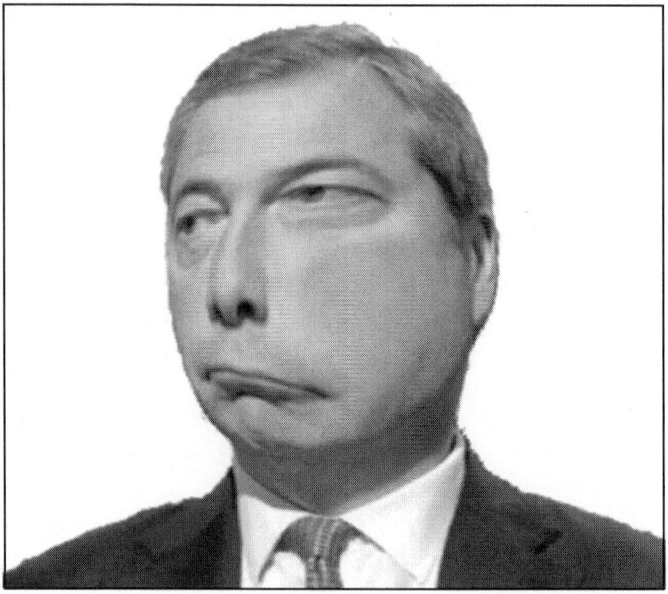

MEP Nikki Sinclaire, who once represented UKIP, stunned Mr Farage by asking whether he should be using taxpayers' cash to employ his alleged love interests.

Miss Sinclaire, Britain's first transgender parliamentarian, said: "Does Mr Farage think it is a fair use of taxpayers' money, namely his secretarial allowance, not only for him to employ his wife Kirsten but his former mistress Annabelle Fuller? Is this a responsible use of UK taxpayers' money?"

Mr Farage, 49, who denies the affair, was given an opportunity to reply but said: "I don't want to answer that at all, thank you."

Mrs Farage said: "Nigel's just on his way back from Strasbourg and we will be discussing it tonight, I'm sure.

Tom McTague, Mirror News

Speaking to Fox News about Obama:

"The guy is a deluded idiot!"

Nigel Farage

When Godfrey Bloom MEP, infamous for making a speech in the European Parliament – one of his better ones – while heavily intoxicated, said that "no employer with a brain in the right place would employ a young, single, free woman", Farage's reaction was "Dear old Godders!"

Alex Andreou, New Statesman

Sitting in the sunshine on the restaurant's pavement terrace enabled Mr Farage to indulge in two of his many politically incorrect pleasures: smoking (he got through half a dozen cigarettes, breaking off to buy another pack after the main course, complaining 'bloody £8.80 that cost me, outrageous!'); and taunting climate change zealots – he cosied up to a giant patio heater, blamed by many for adding to global warming, scoffing: 'People like Prince Charles talk such nonsense.'

Simon Walters, Mail Online

When Dermot Murnaghan read a quotation to Nigel Farage about the effects of immigration on "indigenous" Britons, the UKIP leader agreed with it, only to be told that the words came from Enoch Powell's infamous "rivers of blood" speech. Undaunted, he endorsed Powell's "basic principle". Indeed Farage remembers even as a schoolboy giving "spirited defences" of a man who called for the repatriation of non-white people.

                          Leo Benedictus The Guardian

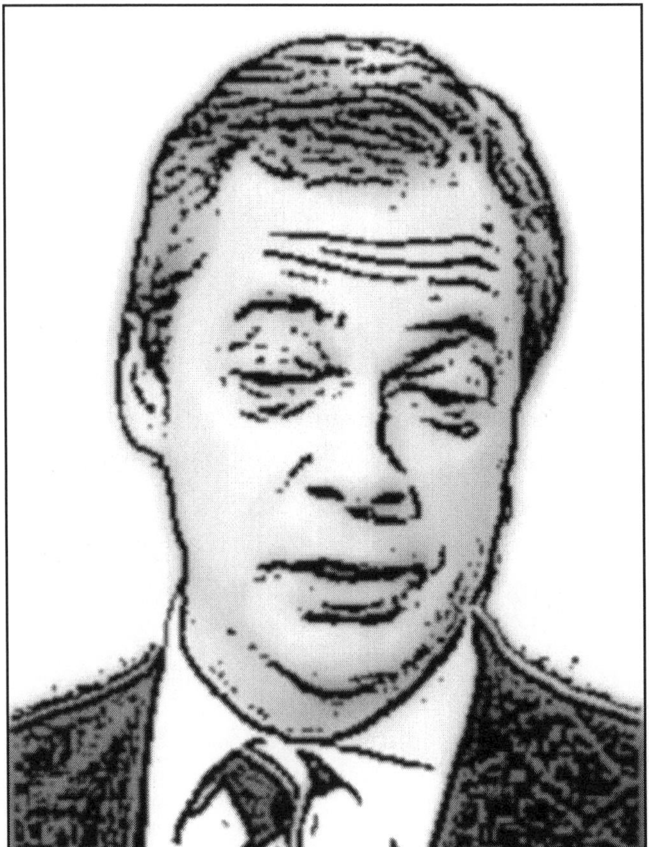

"But there's certainly only one thing I could never agree with George Galloway on. He's a teetotaller and wants to close all the bars in the House of Commons. That is just not on."

Nigel Farage

"If an idea is indeed sensible, it will eventually become just part of the accepted wisdom."

Nigel Farage

Writing about food he ate when he was four:

"There were also ingenious sardines which had somehow escaped their tins. The correct masculine thing here was to crunch them, bones, burned skins and all, whilst females and infants grimaced and said ooh.

"I already knew my role. Because my dad, my glamorous, beautifully dressed, funny, generous, adventurous dad - well, what else could all those prolonged absences mean save adventure? – was my model, I crunched the skin and bones and said that it was good, and was rewarded for being like him with some strange lemony biscuits which seemed to be called lavatories."

Nigel Farage, in his book: Flying Free

"I remember the first time I interviewed Mr Farage, years ago, before he had anything like a national presence. I asked him how to pronounce his name. 'What do you put your car in?' he asked me. 'Well I put my car in a garage,' I retorted, pronouncing the last syllable to rhyme with what UKIP housewives are supposed to clean behind. He looked rather crestfallen."

Cathy Newman, Presenter, Channel 4

"An ungenerous, backwards looking politics has emerged in Britain. The politics of blame has found an acceptable face: it wears a big smile and looks like someone you could have a pint with down the pub."

Nick Clegg about Nigel Farage

Speaking about David Cameron's speech on Britain's relationship with the European Union:

"We wouldn't want to be like the Swiss, would we? That would be awful! We'd be rich!"

Nigel Farage

Speaking to TV presenter Andrew Neil:

"Under the last leadership, at the 2010 election, we managed to produce a manifesto that was 486 pages long. You can quote me all sorts of bits from it I won't know, which is why I've said none of it stands today and we will launch it all after the European elections."

Nigel Farage

Accepting his Insurgent of the Year award at The Spectator's Parliamentarian of the Year Awards:

"And I'm jolly well going to make sure that in the European election of next year many more of you despise me, UKIP and the many millions that are going to vote for us."

Nigel Farage

Letter from Godfrey Bloom to The Times

Sir, following your articles about UKIP, I would like to make clear that I am as partial to crumpet as the next man, just not as much as Farage.

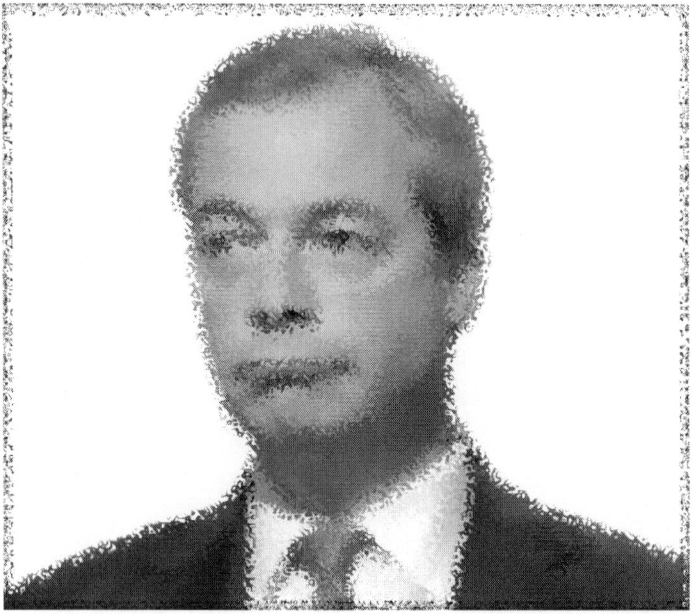

"Now if you look around the UK you will see there are outbreaks of sometimes barmy extremist views from people of all political persuasions. In Whitby, the sun was apparently briefly obscured by a UFO after a Labour councillor claimed to have fathered a child with an extraterrestrial. He also says his real mother is a nine-foot green alien with eight fingers."

Nigel Farage

To the European Parliament:

"I want you all fired!"

Nigel Farage

Spoof quote from Nigel Farage in News Thump

"If you're frustrated with the level of immigration in this country, and feel helpless about it – have you thought about how much more empowered you might feel by owning a gun? If so, you should consider voting UKIP."

"Right now the Constitution is mere paper, with no bearing upon the British people, although they might find it good for doorstops, good for real fires and good for fish and chips."

Nigel Farage

Speaking at the EU Parliament about Baroness Cathy Ashton's appointment as High Representative for Foreign Affairs:

"[She] really is the true representation of the modern day political class. In some ways she's ideal, isn't she? She's never had a proper job and she's never been elected to anything in her life, so I guess she's perfect for this European Union."

Nigel Farage

Speaking to Herman Van Rompuy:

"You appear to have a loathing for the very concept of the existence of nation states - perhaps that's because you come from Belgium, which is pretty much a non-country."

Nigel Farage

When asked if he would like to apologise after calling Herman Van Rompuy a 'low-grade bank clerk':

"The only people I'm going to apologise to are bank clerks the world over - if I've offended them then I'm very sorry indeed."

Nigel Farage

Jerzy Buzek ,the president, in 2010, of the European Parliament, when Nigel Farage was fined after refusing to apologise for the personal criticism of Mr Van Rompuy:

"I defend absolutely Mr Farage's right to disagree about the policy or institutions of the Union, but not to personally insult our guests in the European Parliament or the country from which they may come. His behaviour towards Mr Rompuy was inappropriate, unparliamentary and insulting to the dignity of the house."

Before going head to head with Nick Clegg in a debate about Europe:

"I'll say, 'Come on Nick, tell me why you think British people want the EU flag, anthem and Mr Rumpy Pumpy [president of the European council Herman Van Rompuy] – I'm all ears.' Clegg's European at heart, not British."

Nigel Farage

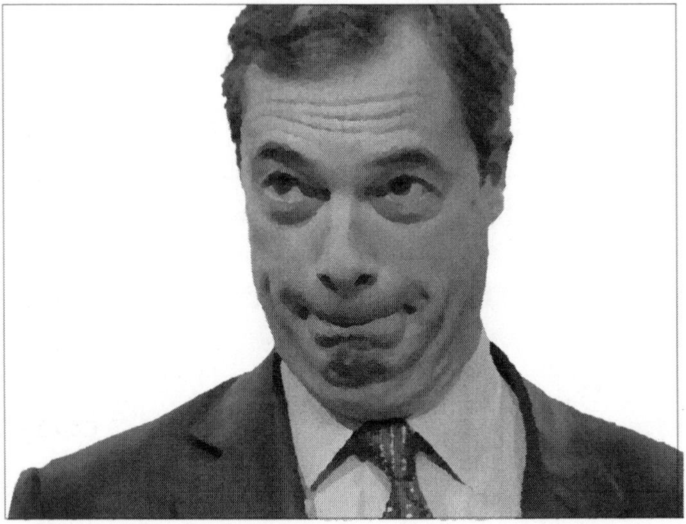

Farage says his party has made patriotism respectable again, but is accused of looking back to a monocultural UK. He said:

"I'm getting a bit tired of my kids coming home from school being taught about every other religion in the world, celebrating every other religious holiday, but not actually being taught about Christianity."

Nigel Farage

"I nearly choked on my bacon roll when I heard Nick Clegg say he wanted to have a debate. I've no choice, I've got to say yes, because we need to have a national debate."

Nigel Farage

Talking about wind farms:

"I'd like to blow them all up. I don't think I've ever seen a single issue in my life more insanely stupid than despoiling our green and pleasant land and our seascapes with ugly bird- and bat-chomping monsters that don't work."

Nigel Farage

Conservative MP Anna Soubry, speaking about Nigel Farage

"I always think he looks like somebody has put their finger up his bottom and he really rather likes it."

Peter Hitchens, writing in The American Spectator, about Nigel Farage:

Experts on English vocal snobbery would instantly be able to tell that he is not, as they say "out of the top drawer." He looks like a frog who has long ago given up hope of being kissed by a princess, and doesn't much mind.

"The EU wants the ability and wants the power when it's tracking our cars as they travel across Europe, if they don't like what we are doing they would have something built in to all new cars that would allow them to press a button and literally stop our car from running. Can you believe the lengths to which these people are prepared to go?"

Nigel Farage

Nigel Farage to journalist Richard Godwin

"Have you met the cretins we have in Westminster? Do you think we can be worse than that?"

A UK Independence Party (UKIP) local election candidate suspended over a photo apparently showing him giving a Nazi salute was in fact doing an impression of a pot plant, Nigel Farage has said.

Metro

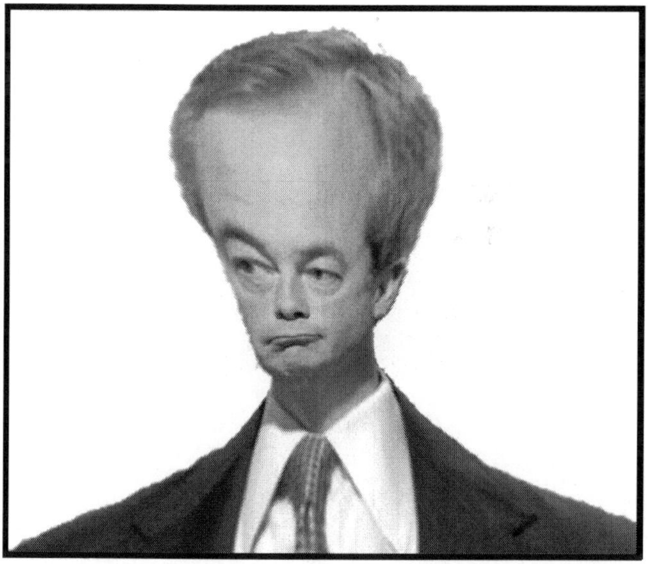

"This job is an unpaid job. It costs a fortune to do. You are on call seven days a week and all you get is aggravation."

Nigel Farage

About UKIP's 2010 manifesto, Nigel Farage said:

"I didn't read it. It was drivel. It was 486 pages of drivel. It was a nonsense."

"Do I think parts of Britain are a foreign land? I got the train the other night, it was rush hour, from Charing Cross. It was a stopper going out and we stopped at London Bridge, New Cross, Hither Green, it was not till we got past Grove Park that I could hear English being audibly spoken in the carriage. Does that make me feel slightly awkward? Yes it does. I wonder what is really going on. I am saying that and I am sure that is a view that will be reflected by three quarters of the population, perhaps even more."

Nigel Farage

"I'm not saying that people on trains should be forced to speak English. That's a bloody stupid question."

Nigel Farage

When answering questions at UKIP's spring conference:

Q: Why did you feel uncomfortable when you were on a train and people were not speaking English?

Farage: "Because I didn't understand them."

Q: So they should speak more English?

Farage: "No, they should speak English."

Part of an interview between LBC's Radio interviewer and Nigel Farage after O'Brien asked him if he felt uncomfortable when his wife and daughters speak German:

Farage: "No, because they can speak English … If you look at the primary school situation in the east end of London, where you've now got schools where a majority don't speak English …"

O'Brien: "The children you refer to are recorded as having English as a second language … Your own children would fit into that category … You felt uncomfortable about people speaking foreign languages, despite the fact that presumably your own wife does when she phones home to Germany."

Farage: (in an exasperated tone of voice): "I don't suppose she speaks it on the train."

Replying to a question from Denis MacShane about his expenses and allowances as an MEP:

"It is a vast sum… I don't know what the total amount is but - oh lor - it must be pushing £2 million."

"I'm not really a politician at all, of course. That's the extraordinary thing. Almost everybody in politics today, from about the age of 14 or 15, they want to be politicians. They have this career path. They are absolutely career politicians. I never had any intention of being involved in this at all."

Nigel Farage

(He joined the Conservative Party at the age of 14)

"I've been in the European Parliament for fifteen years and I have never once voted."

Nigel Farage

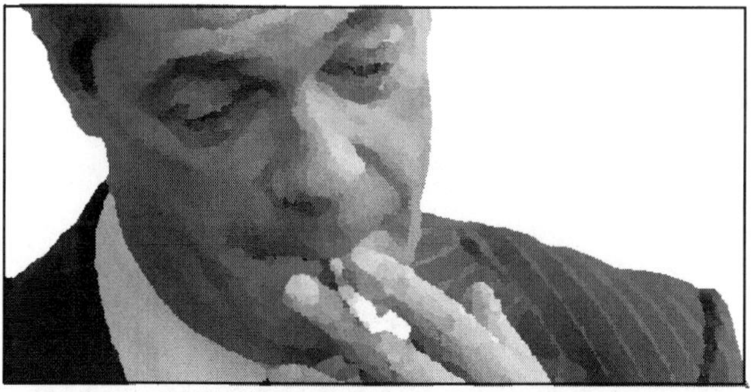

George Parker, FT Magazine

Farage is a heavy consumer of Rothmans cigarettes and enjoys sea-fishing and country sports. A Barbour-clad Farage loves cricket and used to be seen enjoying hare coursing – until it was banned in 2005. In short, he is a young-ish fogey: most people are surprised to learn he is still in his forties.

Prince Charles received a standing ovation from about 150 British MEPs and representatives from the European Parliament's climate change and environment committees. But Nigel Farage remained seated.

"How can somebody like Prince Charles be allowed to come to the European Parliament at this time to announce he thinks it should have more powers? It would have been better for the country he wants to rule one day if he had stayed home and tried to persuade Gordon Brown to give the people the promised referendum on the Treaty of Lisbon."

Nigel Farage

The leader of the UK Labour Party's MEPs, Gary Titley said:

"I was embarrassed and disgusted when the Leader of the UK Independence Party, Nigel Farage, remained firmly seated during the lengthy standing ovation Prince Charles received. I had not realised Mr Farage's blind adherence to right wing politics involved disloyalty and discourtesy to the Royal Family. He should be thoroughly ashamed of himself and should apologise to the British people he represents."

Nigel Farage on Prince Charles' European speech:

It reminded me of young Mr Grace in that old TV series, "Are You Being Served?"

Asked by Mr Campbell to say "something nice" about the three major party leaders, the normally garrulous Mr Farage was almost lost for words, describing each of them as "nice".

Mr Cameron is "a perfectly nice fellow who stands four-square for nothing," Mr Miliband a "nice chap, not very worldly - I would love to see him in a working men's club in Newcastle", while Liberal Democrat leader Nick Clegg - who took on Mr Farage in a TV debate last week - was a "very nice guy, just wrong".

A letter from former teacher, Chloe Deakin, claims that Farage and others had once

"marched through a quiet Sussex village very late at night shouting Hitler-youth songs".

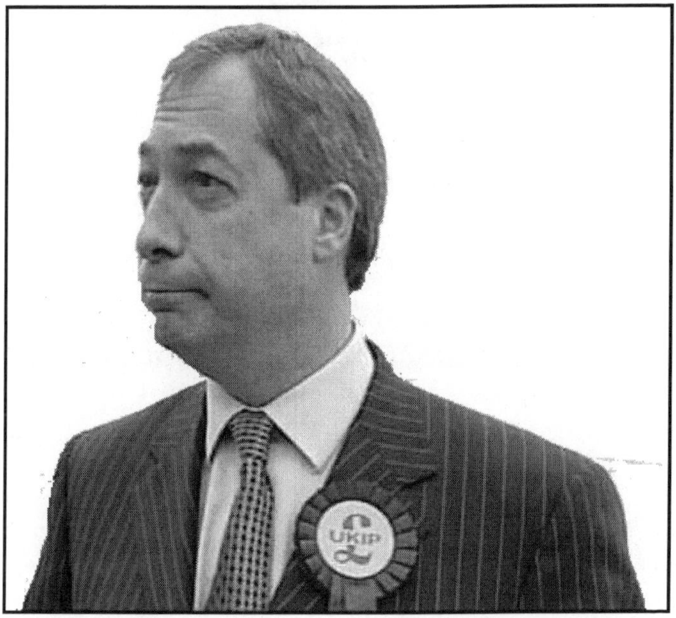
UKIP

About the Environment agency:

"…whose priorities appear to be more concerned on the preservation of molluscs, beetles and water voles than our farmer and our householders; compliance with EU directives being more important than flood prevention."

Nigel Farage

About Neil Hamilton:

"He's the back room boy, he's the campaign manager... When it comes to claims from journalists about what he did or did not do, I generally find ... I remember being told he was convicted of something, which I don't believe he was.

He's our campaign manager, whatever happened in the past is the past, he's not the front face of the party but he is fulfilling an important role helping us get this campaign organised ...

There are things that went wrong in his career, we all have things in our life that have gone wrong, that's the way it is."
Nigel Farage

Hamilton, when asked if he was just a backroom boy, told BBC's Newnight that he considered himself "front-of-house".

Journalist, Ned Simons, writes in the Huffington Post:

The UKIP leader has been accused of a racial slur after commenting that people should be concerned if a group of Romanians moved in next door to them. Asked by LBC Radio why it would be ok for Germans to move in and not Romanians was, he replied: "You know what the difference is."...

(David) Lammy, the MP for Tottenham said on Monday: "What Nigel Farage said over the weekend was racist. So I'm clear, he's a racist..."

...UKIP took out a full-page advertisement in a national newspaper to insist the party was not racist but repeated its warning about the risk posed by organised criminal gangs from Romania. Farage said his comments about people being right to be concerned if a group of Romanian men moved in next door had caused a "predictable storm of protest and accusations of racism".

Ed Miliband:

"Nigel Farage is not racist but his comments are deeply offensive."

Farage chuckles at the idea that he does not like women. In 2006 he drunkenly suspended his hostility to the EU's open borders policy to accept an invitation for a late-night drink from a "sleek and seductive" 25-year-old Latvian called Lita.

Lita told the News of the World that Farage was something of a stud and that they had had sex seven times before he fell asleep, "snoring like a horse".

George Parker, FT Magazine

Talking about women and work

"If a woman with a client base has a child and takes two or three years off work, she is worth far less to the employer when she comes back than when she goes away because her client base cannot be stuck rigidly to her."

Nigel Farage

"Maybe it's because I've got so many women pregnant over the years that I have a different view [of maternity leave]."

Nigel Farage

"It's a European Union of economic failure, of mass unemployment and of low growth."

Nigel Farage

"Greece isn't a democracy now it's run through a troika - three foreign officials that fly into Athens airport and tell the Greeks what they can and can't do."

Nigel Farage

"When people stand up and talk about the great success that the EU has been, I'm not sure anybody saying it really believes it themselves anymore."

Nigel Farage

"I think frankly when it comes to chaos you ain't seen nothing yet."

> Nigel Farage

"I have become increasingly used to the Tory party mimicking our policies and phrases in a desperate effort to pretend to their members they are still Eurosceptic."

Nigel Farage

"I think that politics needs a bit of spicing up."

                                            Nigel Farage

Boris Johnson, Mayor of London says of Nigel Farage:

"A rather engaging geezer. He's anti-pomposity, he's anti-political correctness, he's anti-loony Brussels regulation. He's in favour of low tax, sticking up for small business and sticking up for Britain. We Tories look at him, with his pint and cigar and sense of humour, and instinctively recognise someone fundamentally indistinguishable from us."

Speaking about Boris Johnson

"He's the only Tory politician who UKIP members listen to and agree [with] much of what he has to say."

Nigel Farage

About Douglas Carswell, former Tory MP for Clacton who resigned his seat to join UKIP thus forcing a by-election

"So if Douglas Carswell wins this by-election and those backbench MPs with a favourable view of UKIP believe they are more likely to win their seats as UKIP than as Tory or Labour, then more will follow.

"The Clacton by-election is of huge significance not just to the future of UKIP but to the whole of British politics. It will indeed be our high noon."

Nigel Farage

Comments about Romanian immigrants

"I do not wish for people to feel in a discriminatory manner towards Romanians but I do say there is a very real problem here, that everybody else has run away from, brushed under the carpet, the whole organised crime element and the impact that has had on London and other parts of the country. That is a serious issue."

Nigel Farage

Kirsten Farage worries about her husband, Nigel. Here are some of her comments:

"He doesn't get a lot of sleep, he doesn't get a lot of rest, he lives on adrenaline a lot, he doesn't eat regular meals, now I am beginning to sound like his mother, and he smokes and he drinks too much.

"But if you have that sort of lifestyle I think it is what keeps him going, it keeps the adrenaline going."

"When he is out and about, he is noisy and extrovert and all this. And [when] you come home you have to put your feet up, and cut the grass and put the bins out.

"He loves fishing, he loves walking, we live in quite a rural area so he can literally walk out and you have got fields and you have got valleys.

"Apart from that he used to play a lot of golf but that was before my day, and before UKIP. Now he hasn't got time for it.

"We honestly don't watch a lot of telly but he loves Dads' Army, he loves all the 70s stuff that they still repeat."

"We seek an amicable divorce from the European Union and its replacement with a genuine free-trade agreement, which is what my parents' generation thought we'd signed up for in the first place."

Nigel Farage

Speaking on BBC Radio Scotland after being forced to take refuge in a pub during the Scottish Independence referendum:

"The fact 50 yobbo fascist scum turn up and aren't prepared to listen to the debate, I refuse to believe is representative of public opinion."

Nigel Farage

"The euro Titanic has now hit the iceberg - and there simply aren't enough lifeboats to go round."

Nigel Farage

"Once again, I challenge the Prime Minister to have an open debate with me on why he believes we must stay part of this failing, corrupt EU. The future of our nation is at stake. Mr Cameron, you have my phone number."

Nigel Farage

During an interview with Jason Cowley, New Satesman editor:

Cowley: Would you go into coalition with Labour?

Farage: I'd do a deal with the devil if he got me what I wanted.

"We must break up the Eurozone. We must set those Mediterranean countries free."

Nigel Farage

"The great and the good will decide what is good for us and make sure that we get what is good for us, good and hard."

Nigel Farage

"It's amazing how ideas start out, isn't it?"

Nigel Farage

"Minimum sales prices for alcohol are a startlingly bad idea. As with excise duties, the effects are regressive."

Nigel Farage

"I believe I can lead this party from the front as a campaigning organization."

Nigel Farage

"Before, Europe was about treaties, laws and our sovereign right to govern ourselves. Now, it's about everyday lives.

"It's about mass immigration at a time when 21% of young people can't find work. It's about giving £50million a day to the EU when the public finances are under great strain.

"It's about businesses nervous about taking on school leavers because of a mass of red tape. It's about health and safety regulations and green fines."

Nigel Farage

"I have been unsure, from the start, what the Occupy movement was all about, although I did suspect that it was just fatuous, anti-enterprise, left-wingery."

Nigel Farage

"I have invested the best part of my adult political life in helping to try to build up this movement and I am far from perfect but I do think I am able, through the media, to deliver a good, simple, understandable message."

Nigel Farage

"We have a Conservative leader that believes in green taxes, that won't bring back grammar schools, that believes in continuing with total open-door migration from eastern Europe and refuses to give us a referendum on the EU."

Nigel Farage

"British chancellor is telling the rest of Europe it must abandon democracy. It's appalling."

Nigel Farage

"Having established that good ideas do indeed come in from the cold, start on the fringes and become mainstream, can we make any predictions about what the next move will be?"

Nigel Farage

"If I was a Greek citizen I'd be out there trying to bring down this monstrosity that has been put upon those people."

Nigel Farage

"When an Occupy demo in the centre of Frankfurt makes world news, I shall hurry to join in."

Nigel Farage

Speaking on Sky News about immigrant NHS workers:

"I don't know about you, whether you have even been to a GP who doesn't speak very good English, but it's something that people out there are talking about.

"If people don't speak English and they are dealing with English-speaking patients surely they shouldn't be employed in the first place.

"Don't we want to live in a country where we speak the same language and isn't it scandalous that we are not training enough nurses and doctors in our own country?"

Nigel Farage

On his New Year resolution to take a break from alcohol:

"I started before the new year. I'm not being particularly virtuous, it's just I need a break. It does us all good to have a break now and then."

Nigel Farage

"I don't see Ukip being joined together with Labour and the SNP at all, I really don't.
"In fact, I regard it, even if we were in that position, as unlikely that Ukip would want to be in coalition with anybody. But what you can do is give support to minority governments in return for what you want.

"David Cameron doesn't like Ukip and he doesn't like me and he's been incredibly rude about us over a very long period of time – not just about us personally, but about our policies, saying how appalling they are. And yet now in interviews, he tries to sound a little bit like us.

"Don't forget just two and a bit years ago, Cameron was implacably opposed to having a referendum. Ukip started to do well in one or two by-elections, he changed his tune.

"We would not even be discussing a European referendum if Ukip hadn't done well; if you really want a referendum, make sure there are enough Ukip MPs in Westminster to hold the balance of power."

Nigel Farage

Speaking on BBC Wales, Sunday Politics programme:

"It took me six hours and 15 minutes to get here – it should have taken three-and-a-half to four.

"That is nothing to do with professionalism, what it does have to do with is a population that is going through the roof chiefly because of open-door immigration and the fact that the M4 is not as navigable as it used to be."

Nigel Farage

About the Eurozone crisis:

"It's desperately sad. Inevitably, this is going to end in some kind of widespread violence, the likes of which none of us wants to see. We're not going to be digging holes in Belgium, facing each other, no. But will we get terrorist groups emerging in Greece, Spain and Portugal? Yes."

Nigel Farage

"I've always liked to be the odd one out, wherever I am."

Nigel Farage

On Islam :

"I just have this huge admiration for what the Aussies have done... If you listen to John Howard and what other PMs have said in the past 10 years, of Islam ... he said: 'You're welcome to come here and have your children here... but if you're coming here to take us over, you're not welcome.'"

Nigel Farage

To journalist Alan Roden about UKIP voters:

"Most of you have thought for years that every Ukip voter is a retired half colonel living on the edge of Salisbury plain desperate for the re-introduction for the birch and only cheering up after the first pink gin of the day. Well, we have got a few of those that vote for us there is no doubt about it. But actually we cross all social divides. In terms of geography that's even more fascinating. We have made a breakthrough in Scotland – something which Alex Salmond will not enjoy very much."

Nigel Farage

On the Scottish Independence Referendum:

"I don't even believe this is a referendum on independence, it is a referendum on separation from the United Kingdom. The formula that Salmond is proposing is that they swap Westminster for Brussels. There has not been an open and honest debate about that. There is a segment of Scottish voters who are very pro-Scottish, tempted towards the SNP, tempted towards voting Yes, but who actually when we can point out to them they are being offered a pig and a poke ... will think again."

Nigel Farage

The Breastfeeding Debate

Comments during an interview on LBC about Claridge's hotel request for a mother to cover herself with a cloth, offered to her by a waiter, whilst she was breastfeeding her baby:

"I'm not particularly bothered about it, but I know a lot of people do feel very uncomfortable, and look, this is just a matter of common sense, isn't it? I think that, given that some people feel very embarrassed by it, it isn't too difficult to breastfeed a baby in a way that's not openly ostentatious. Frankly, that's up to Claridge's, and I very much take the view that if you're running an establishment you should have rules."

Nigel Farage

When he was then asked if women should be told to go to the toilet to breastfeed he replied:

"Or perhaps sit in the corner, or whatever it might be – that's up to Claridge's. It's not an issue that I get terribly hung up about, but I know particularly people of the older generation feel awkward and embarrassed by it."

Asked for the Prime Minister's reaction to Farage's comments, David Cameron's spokesperson said:

"It's for Mr Farage to explain his views. The Prime Minister shares the view of the NHS which is that breastfeeding is completely natural and it's totally unacceptable for anybody to be made to feel uncomfortable while breastfeeding in public."

Later, Nigel Farage commented further on the subject of women breastfeeding their babies in public:

"Let me get this clear, as I said on the radio and as I repeat now, I personally have no problem with mothers breastfeeding wherever they want. What I said was - and it is immensely frustrating that I have to explain this - is that if the establishment in question, in this case Claridge's, wants to maintain rules about this stuff, then that is up to them, as it should be. I remarked that perhaps they might ask women to sit in a corner. Did I say I believe they should have to? No. Did I say I personally endorse this concept? No. We do however have to recognise that businesses have a responsibility to all of their customers, some of whom may well be made uncomfortable by public breastfeeding. It's a two-way street: breastfeeding women should never be embarrassed by staff asking them to stop, and most mums will recognise the need to be discreet in certain, limited, circumstances. It's just a question of good manners, and in this case, accurate journalism."

Printed in Great Britain
by Amazon.co.uk, Ltd.,
Marston Gate.